Lessons on Demand Presents

Teacher Guide and Novel Unit for March Book One

By:

John Pennington

The lessons on demand series is designed to provide ready to use resources for novel study. In this book you will find key vocabulary, student organizer pages, and assessments. This guide is divided into two sections. Section one is the teacher section which consists of vocabulary and activities. Section two holds all of the student pages, including assessments and graphic organizers.

Now available! Student Workbooks!

Find them on Amazon.com

Other titles include...

The War That Saved My Life

Esperanza Rising

Walk Two Moons

The Giver

One Crazy Summer

The One and Only Ivan

Flora & Ulysses

Island of the Blue Dolphin

The Little Prince

The Lightning Thief

Where the Red Fern Grows

And more........

Section One

Teacher Pages

Vocabulary

Suggested Activities

Suggested Vocabulary

Conducive

Resistance

Eulogy

Frantic

Desegregation

Injustice

Moral

Philosophy

Liberated

Protest

Instigator

Protest

Activities

Reading Check Question / Quiz:

What did the protestors do on the bridge when confronted by police? They began to pray.

Who inspired John Lewis as a young man on the farm? Dr. King and President Kennedy

What profession did young John Lewis believe he would pursue? Preacher

What was the name of the uncle that opened John Lewis's eyes to a bigger world? Otis Carter.

Blooms Higher Order Question:

Consider what injustices are mentioned in the book. Which ones have improved? Which ones need to continue improving?

Suggested Activity Sheets (see Section Two):

Character Sketch—John Lewis

Character Sketch—Otis Carter

Character Sketch—Jim Lawson

Research Connection—Civil Rights

Research Connection—John Lewis

Research Connection—Rosa Parks

Research Connection—Dr. Martin Luther King Jr.

Research Connection—U. S. Supreme Court

Research Connection—Brown vs. Board of Education

Research Connection—Emmett Till

Chapter Vocabulary

Suggested Activity Sheets (see Section Two):

Research Connection—Gandhi

Compare and Contrast—Love and Hate

Create the Test

Top Ten List—Events

Who, What, When, Where and How

Write a Letter—to John Lewis

Discussion Questions

Does John Lewis seem like a politician?

How does John Lewis's childhood compare to your own?

What are the issues involved in the civil rights movement?

Do we currently have civil rights issues that need to be addressed and what are those issues?

Where are the places you are afraid to go and why?

What places where off limits?

Do nonviolent protests work? How much effort do they take to succeed?

What must you be willing to endure to protest in a nonviolent way?

Reading Check Question / Quiz:

What events inspires John Lewis to get involved in the civil rights movement? The sermon of Dr. Martin Luther King jr.. The trial of Emmett Till, and Rosa Parks.

What school did John Lewis want to attend but was not allowed in? Troy State

What was the initial result of the nonviolent protests? Humiliation, scorn and arrest

Upon being released and asked to give allow changes to be made did they need to continue the protests? Yes the protesting needed to continue.

Additional Vocabulary

Additional Activities

Reading Check Question / Quiz:

Blooms Higher Order Question:

Suggested Activity Sheets (see Section Two):

Discussion Questions

Section Two

Student Work Pages

Work Pages

Graphic Organizers

Assessments

Activity Descriptions

Advertisement—Select an item from the text and have the students use text clues to draw an advertisement about that item.

Chapter to Poem—Students select 20 words from the text to write a five line poem with 3 words on each line.

Character Sketch—Students complete the information about a character using text clues.

Comic Strip— Students will create a visual representation of the chapter in a series of drawings.

Compare and Contrast—Select two items to make relationship connections with text support.

Create the Test—have the students use the text to create appropriate test questions.

Draw the Scene—students use text clues to draw a visual representation of the chapter.

Interview— Students design questions you would ask a character in the book and then write that characters response.

Lost Scene—Students use text clues to decide what would happen after a certain place in the story.

Making Connections—students use the text to find two items that are connected and label what kind of relationship connects them.

Precognition Sheet—students envision a character, think about what will happen next, and then determine what the result of that would be.

Activity Descriptions

Pyramid—Students use the text to arrange a series of items in an hierarchy format.

Research Connection—Students use an outside source to learn more about a topic in the text.

Sequencing—students will arrange events in the text in order given a specific context.

Support This! - Students use text to support a specific idea or concept.

Travel Brochure—Students use information in the text to create an informational text about the location

Top Ten List—Students create a list of items ranked from 1 to 10 with a specific theme.

Vocabulary Box—Students explore certain vocabulary words used in the text.

What Would You Do? - Students compare how characters in the text would react and compare that with how they personally would react.

Who, What, When, Where, and How—Students create a series of questions that begin with the following words that are connected to the text.

Write a Letter—Students write a letter to a character in the text.

Activity Descriptions (for scripts and poems)

Add a Character—Students will add a character that does not appear in the scene and create dialog and responses from other characters.

Costume Design—Students will design costumes that are appropriate to the characters in the scene and explain why they chose the design.

Props Needed— Students will make a list of props they believe are needed and justify their choices with text.

Soundtrack! - Students will create a sound track they believe fits the play and justify each song choice.

Stage Directions— Students will decide how the characters should move on, around, or off stage.

Poetry Analysis—Students will determine the plot, theme, setting, subject, tone and important words and phrases.

Advertisement: Draw an advertisement for _____

NAME:

TEACHER:

Date:

Chapter to Poem

Assignment: Select 20 words found in the chapter to create a poem where each line is 3 words long.

Title:

_____ _____ _____

_____ _____ _____

_____ _____ _____

_____ _____ _____

_____ _____ _____

NAME:

TEACHER:

Date:

Character Sketch

Name

Draw a picture

Personality/ Distinguishing marks

Connections to other characters

Important Actions

NAME:

TEACHER:

Date:

Comic Strip

NAME:

TEACHER:

Date:

Compare and Contrast
Venn Diagram

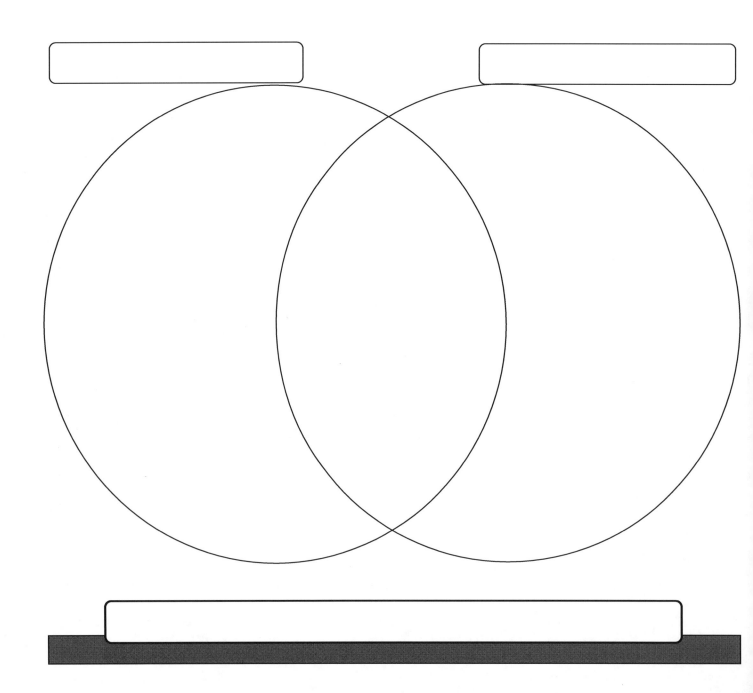

Create the Test

Question:

Answer:

Question:

Answer:

Question:

Answer:

Question:

Answer:

NAME:

TEACHER:

Date:

Draw the Scene: What five things have you included in the scene?

1   2   3

4   5

NAME:

TEACHER:

Date:

Interview: Who _____

Question:

Answer:

Question:

Answer:

Question:

Answer:

Question:

Answer:

Lost Scene: Write a scene that takes place between _____ and

_____

Making Connections

What is the connection?

NAME:

TEACHER:

Date:

Precognition Sheet

Who ?

What's going to happen?

What will be the result?

Who ?

What's going to happen?

What will be the result?

Who ?

What's going to happen?

What will be the result?

Who ?

What's going to happen?

What will be the result?

How many did you get correct?

NAME:

TEACHER:

Date:

Assignment: Pyramid

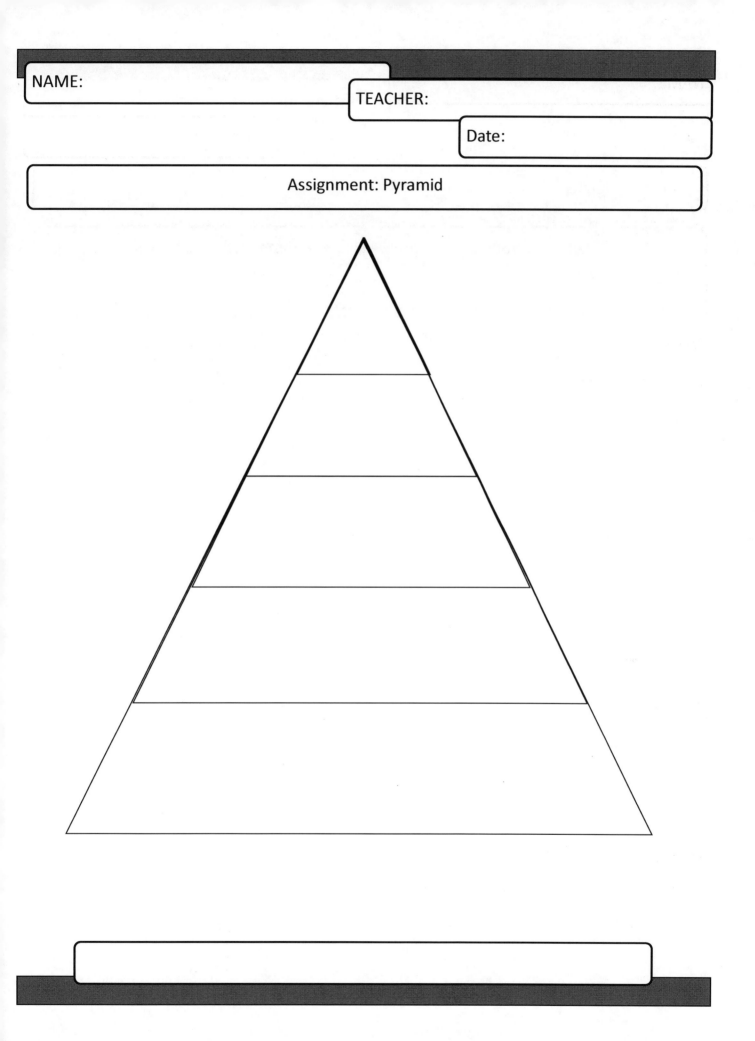

NAME:

TEACHER:

Date:

Research connections

Source (URL, Book, Magazine, Interview)

What am I researching?

Facts I found that could be useful or notes

1.

2.

3.

4.

5.

6.

NAME:

TEACHER:

Date:

1.

Sequencing or timeline

2.

3.

4.

5.

NAME:

Support This!

Supporting text

What page?

Supporting text

What page?

Central idea or statement

_____

Supporting text

What page?

Supporting text

What page?

NAME:

TEACHER:

Date:

Travel Brochure

Why should you visit?

What are you going to see?

Map

Special Events

Top Ten List

1.

2.

3.

4.

5.

6.

7.

8.

9.

10.

NAME:

TEACHER:

Date:

Vocabulary Box

Definition:

Draw:

Word:

Related words:

Use in a sentence:

Definition:

Draw:

Word:

Related words:

Use in a sentence:

NAME:

TEACHER:

Date:

What would you do?

Character: _____

What did they do?

Example from text:

What would you do?

Why would that be better?

Character: _____

What did they do?

Example from text:

What would you do?

Why would that be better?

Character: _____

What did they do?

Example from text:

What would you do?

Why would that be better?

NAME:

TEACHER:

Date:

Who, What, When, Where, and How

Who

What

Where

When

How

NAME:

TEACHER:

Date:

Write a letter

To:

From:

NAME:

TEACHER:

Date:

Assignment:

Add a Character

Who is the new character?

What reason does the new character have for being there?

Write a dialog between the new character and characters currently in the scene.

You dialog must be 6 lines or more, and can occur in the beginning, middle or end of the scene.

NAME:

TEACHER:

Date:

Costume Design

Draw a costume for one the characters in the scene.

Why do you believe this character should have a costume like this?

NAME:

TEACHER:

Date:

Props Needed

Prop:

What text from the scene supports this?

Prop:

What text from the scene supports this?

Prop:

What text from the scene supports this?

NAME:

TEACHER:

Date:

Soundtrack!

Song:

Why should this song be used?

Song:

Why should this song be used?

Song:

Why should this song be used?

NAME:

TEACHER:

Date:

Stage Directions

List who is moving, how they are moving and use text from the dialog to determine when they move.

Who:

How:

When:

Who:

How:

When:

Who:

How:

When:

NAME:

TEACHER:

Poetry Analysis

Date:

Name of Poem:

Subject:

Text Support:

Plot:

Text Support:

Theme:

Text Support:

Setting:

Text Support:

Tone:

Text Support:

Important Words and Phrases:

Why are these words and phrases important:

Made in the USA
Middletown, DE
21 June 2022

67480202R10024